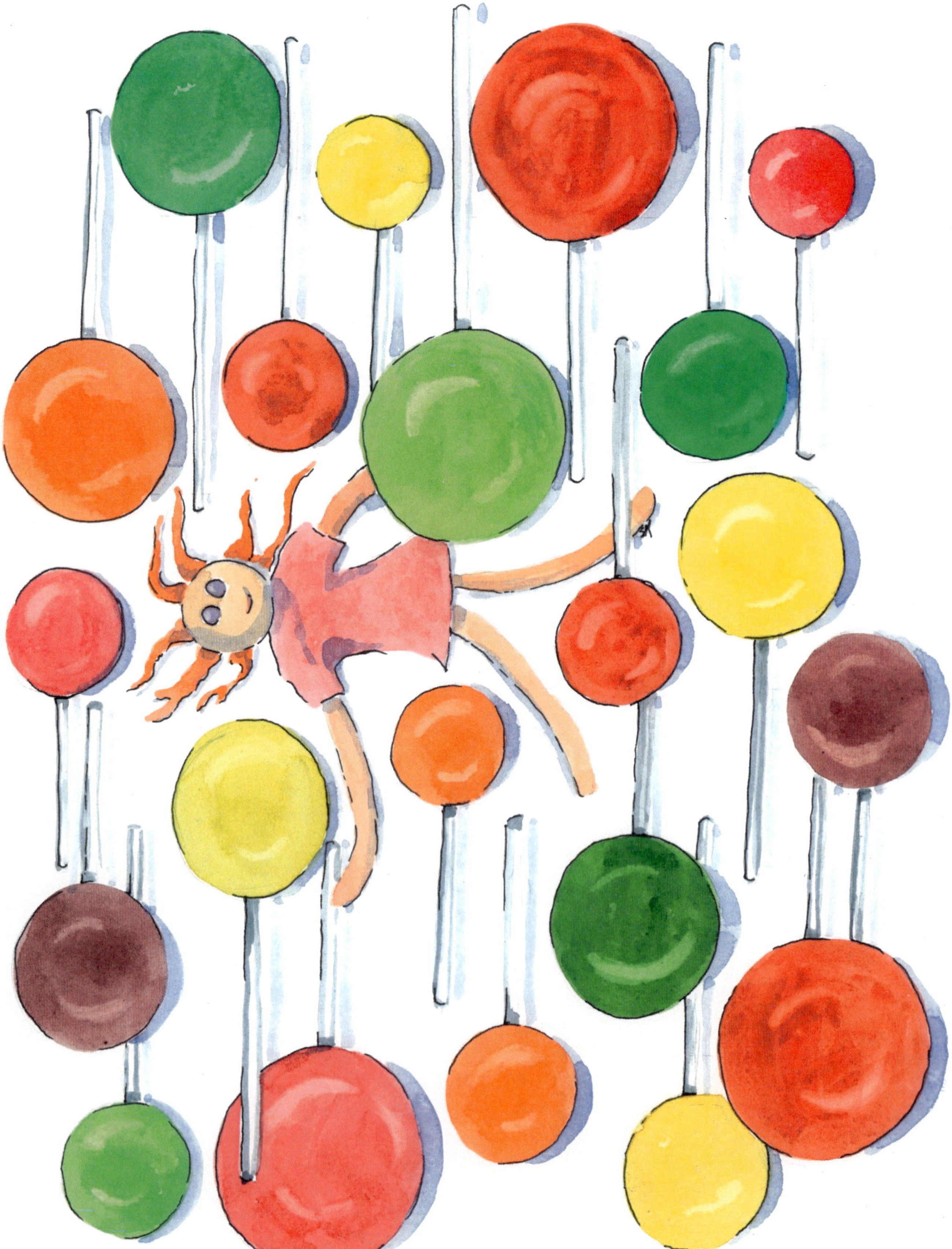

# Locks of Lollipops

## By Kristin Elise Steffen

Locks of Lollipops

By Kristin Elise Steffen

No portion of this work may be transmitted or reproduced in any form without the written permission of the author.

Sara Stoops Robbins, Illustrator

ISBN-10:1516974735

ISBN-13:978-1516974733

Copyright© 2015

Kristin Elise Steffen

# Dedication

By Kristin Elise Steffen

To Masey and Ally, Steffen Sweetheart Alumni.


By Sara Stoops Robbins

To Remy, the artist entertainer and inspiration

and her gorgeous mother, Ernante.

Annabelle was a fairly typical girl. She liked playing with her orange-haired doll, Bridget, wearing leg warmers and going to Sunday School.

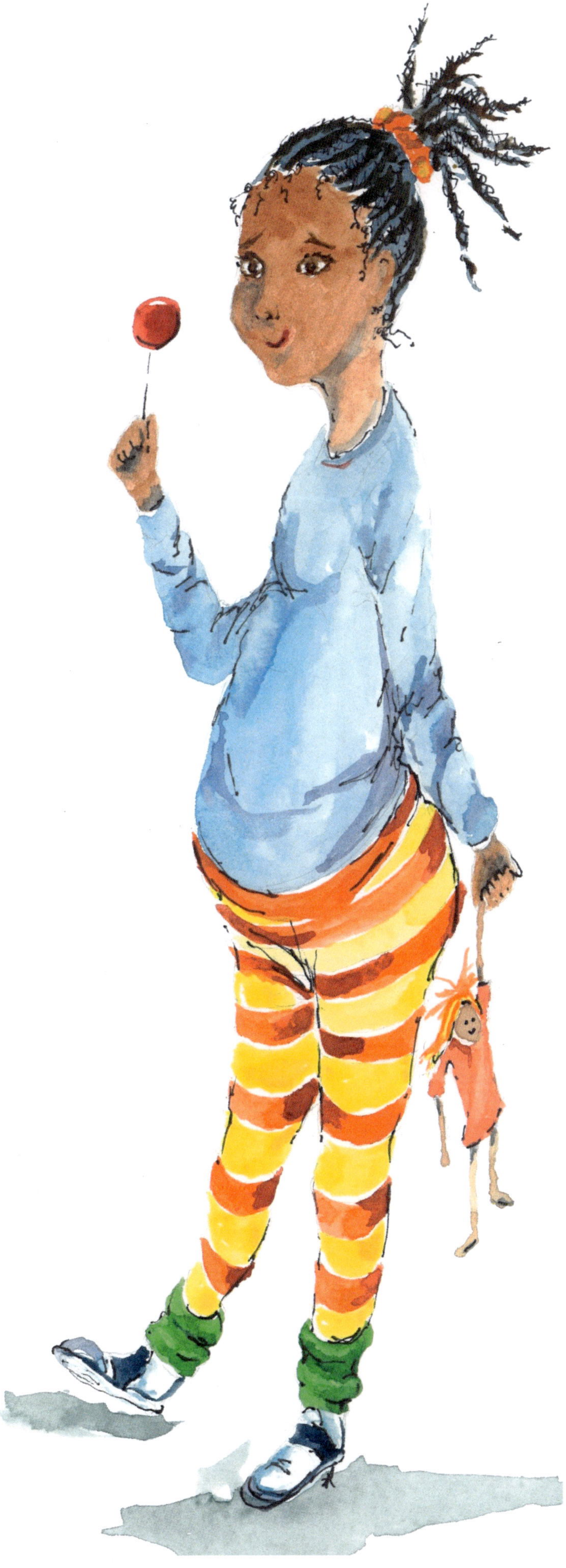

She didn't like spiders—SQUISH, broccoli—BLAH, rainy days, or...

When her brother wouldn't play house, because he was setting up his army men.

But Annabelle was different because she liked lollipops.

That doesn't sound weird, but she liked them so much, she insisted that her mother give her a new lollipop everyday.

Sometimes her mom gave Annabelle a large lollipop!

Every night Annabelle would fall asleep

clutching a half-eaten lollipop

in her hand.

Every morning, the lollipops stuck in her hair and hurt to pull out, and she wouldn't let her mom cut her braids.

After a month, there were so many suckers stuck in her hair that she looked like a lollipop head.

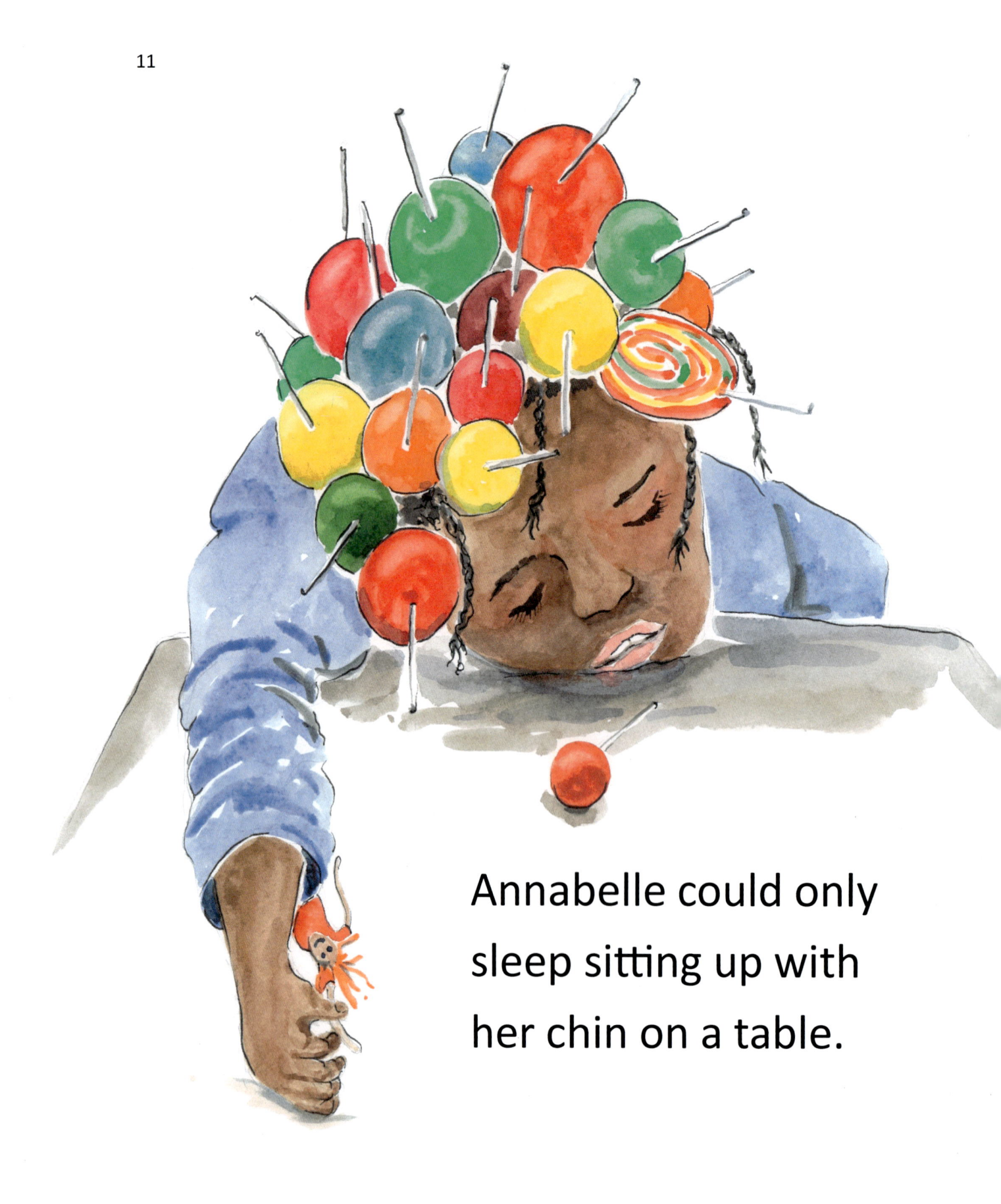

Annabelle could only sleep sitting up with her chin on a table.

Her Grampy, who could make anything from toothpicks and toilet paper, designed a special pillow for Annabelle.

Someone needed to get those lollipops out of her hair, but who? Annabelle, of course! She was really tired of stuck suckers.

She thought a hot shower would work.
You should have seen the colors
run down her legs and onto
the
shower
Floor!

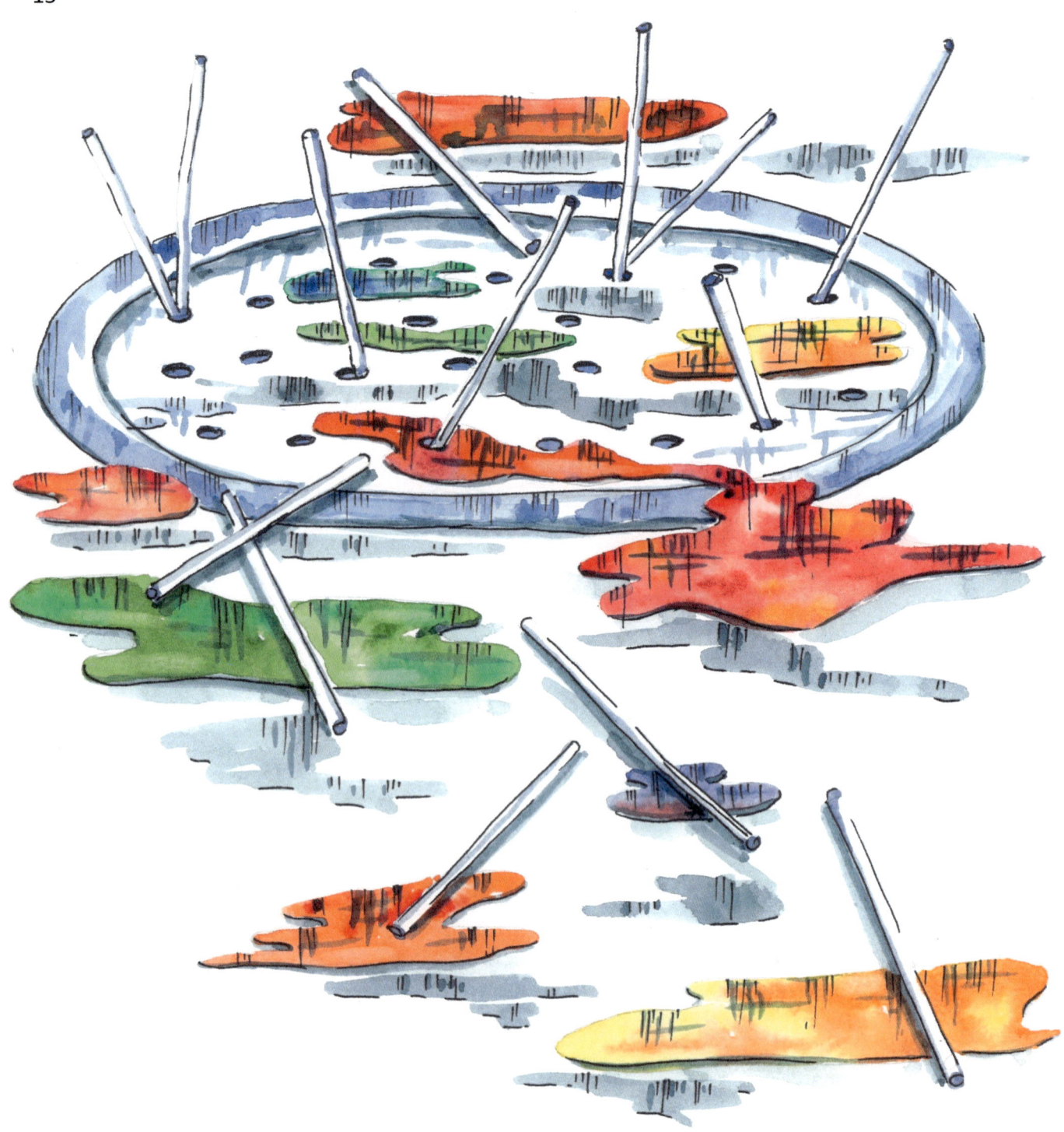

At the end, Annabelle was left with a drain of sticks, puddles of color and ...

...a new hairdo! And now,

..she loves bubble gum!  Uh oh!

18

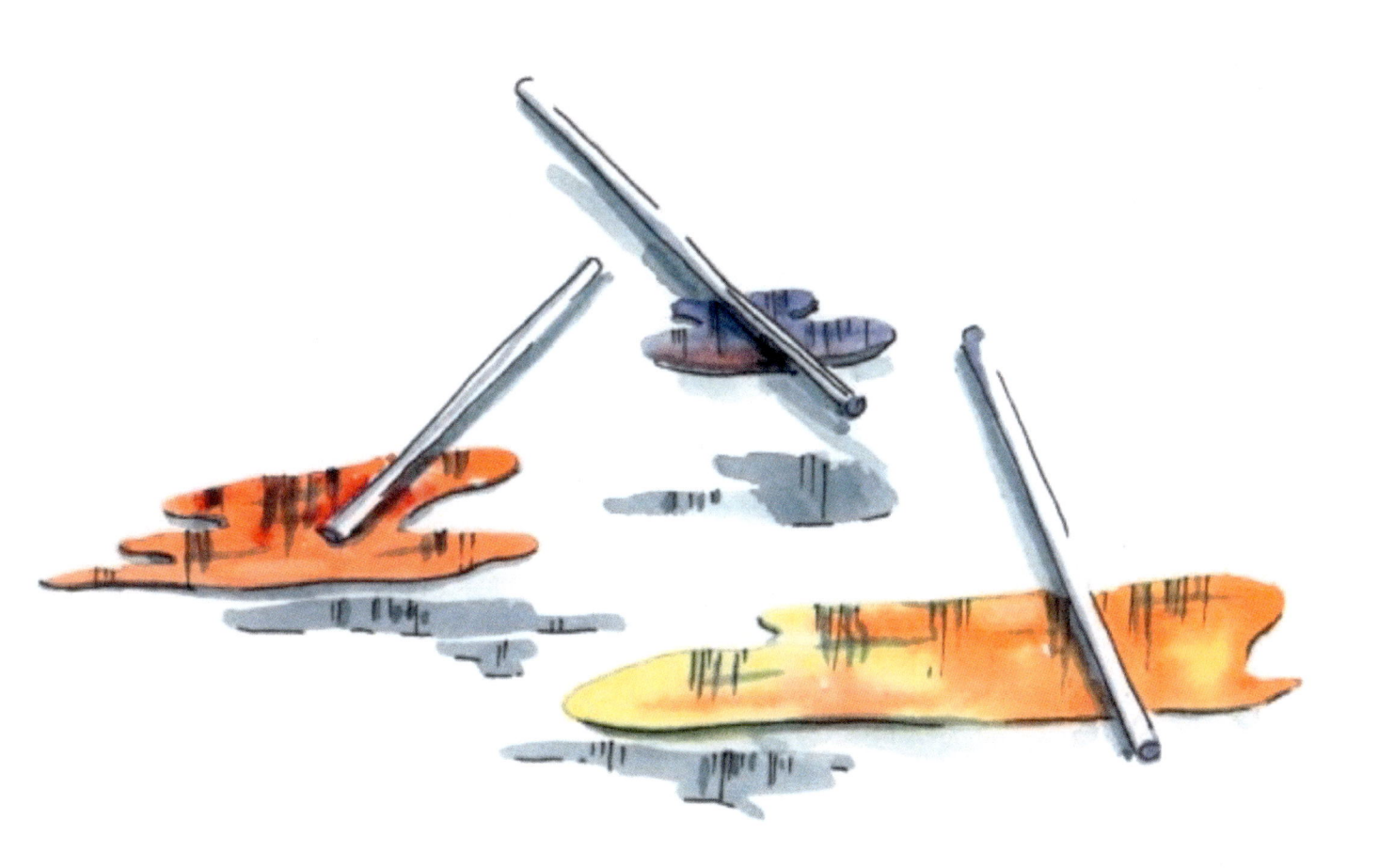

## Author

**Kristin Elise Steffen** and her husband divide their time between Indiana, the Blue Ridge Mountains of North Carolina and Florida. They have two grown daughters, a son-in-law and one grimalkin named Sugar.

## Illustrator

**Sara Stoops Robbins** has made art for over 50 years and taught art for 30 years. She is married to Joel, a writer and teacher, and they are blessed with two children and four grandchildren. They occasionally babysit one obnoxious Creamsicle cat named Sugar.

Made in the USA
Monee, IL
23 December 2024